Chasing Pavements

Words & Music by Adele Adkins & Eg White

THE BEST OF
ADELE

12 HIT SONGS ARRANGED
FOR EASY PIANO

Wise Publications
part of The Music Sales Group

London / New York / Paris / Sydney / Copenhagen /
Berlin / Madrid / Hong Kong / Tokyo

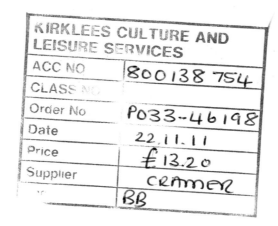

8

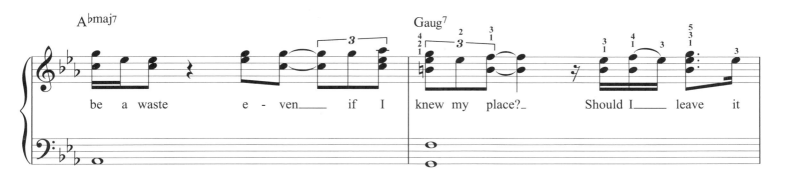

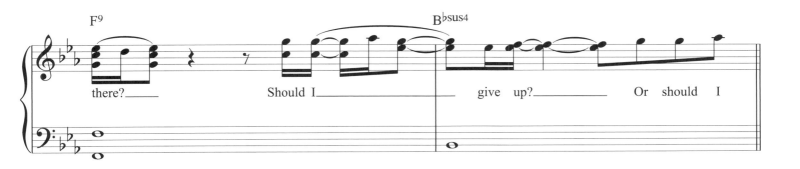

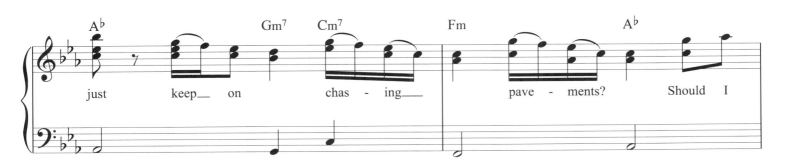

D.S. al Coda

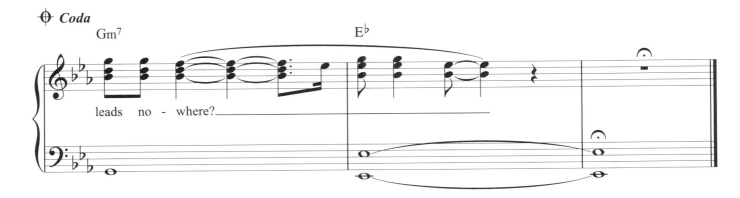

Cold Shoulder

Words & Music by Adele Adkins

To Coda ⊕

11

13

Daydreamer

Words & Music by Adele Adkins

15

16

17

But I will

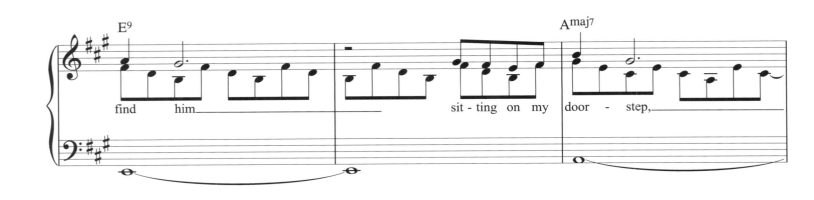

find him_____ sit - ting on my door - step,_____

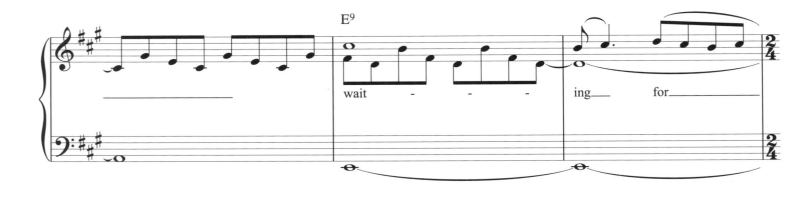

_____ wait - - - - ing_____ for_____

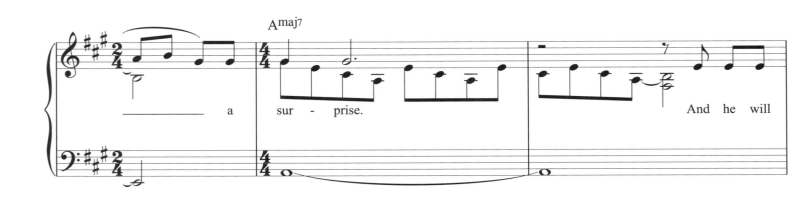

_____ a sur - prise. And he will

18

feel like he's been there for hours,_____

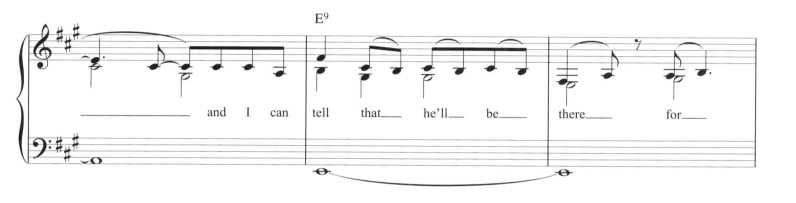

_____ and I can tell that___ he'll___ be___ there___ for___

life.___ And I can tell that___ he'll be

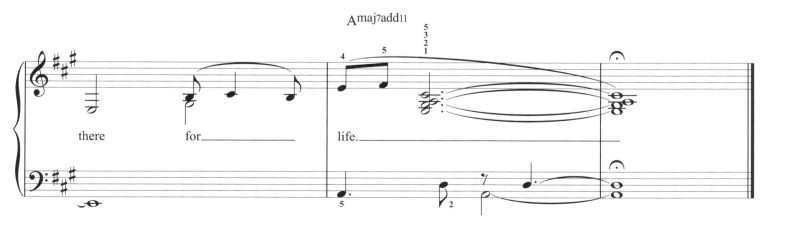

there for_____ life._____

Don't You Remember

Words & Music by Daniel Wilson & Adele Adkins

1. When will I see you_____ a - gain?_____ You left with

2. When was the last time that you thought of me?_____ Or have you com-

no good - bye. Not a sin - gle word__ was said. No

-plete - ly e - rased me from your__ mem - o - ry? I of - ten

fi - nal kiss to seal____ an - y sins.____ I had
think a - bout where I went wrong.____ The more I

no i - dea of the state___ we were in.____ I know I have a
do_____ the less I___ know.___ I know I have a

fick - le heart and a bit - ter - ness. And a wond'ring eye___ and a heav - i - ness in my__ head._

___ But don't you re - mem - ber?____

21

Don't you re - mem - ber

the rea-son you loved me be - fore? Ba - by, please re-mem -

- ber me once more.

more.

Gave you the space so you could breath. I kept my dis-tance so you would be free. In

Hometown Glory

Words & Music by Adele Adkins

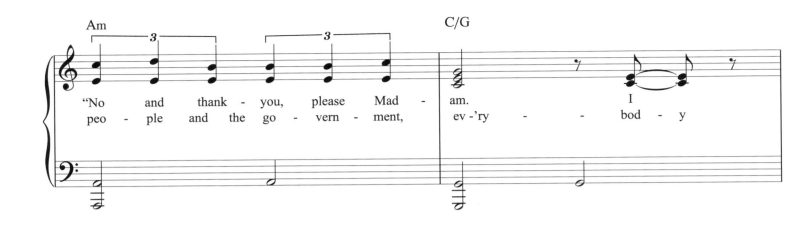

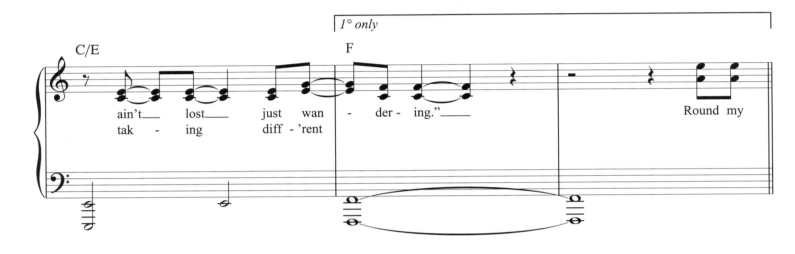

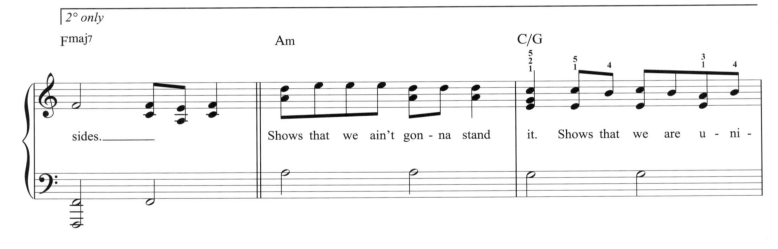

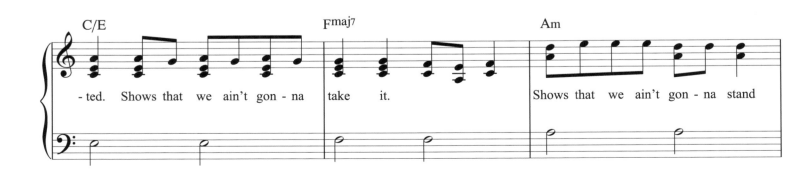

it. Shows that we are u - ni - ted.___ Round my

home - town   mem - - o - ries___ are fresh.___

___   Round my home - town,   oh,___   the

peo - ple I've___ met___   are the won - ders of my___
2° vocal ad lib.

___ world,___   are the won - ders of my___

29

Make You Feel My Love

Words & Music by Bob Dylan

1. When the rain___ is blow - ing___ in your face,___
2. When the eve - ning shad - ows and the___ stars ap - pear,___

and the whole world is on your case,
and there is no one there to dry your tears,

I could of - fer you a warm em - brace
I could hold you for a mil - lion years

to make you feel my love.
to make you feel my love.

I know you have - n't made your mind up yet,
The storms are rag - ing on the roll - ing sea,

but I would nev - er do you wrong.
and on the high - way of re - gret

31

to make you feel my love.
to make you feel my love,

Instrumental

To Coda ⊕

D.S. al Coda

⊕ *Coda*

rit.

to make you feel my love.

33

Right As Rain

Words & Music by J Silverman, Adele Adkins & Leon Michels

37

Rolling In The Deep

Words & Music by Adele Adkins & Paul Epworth

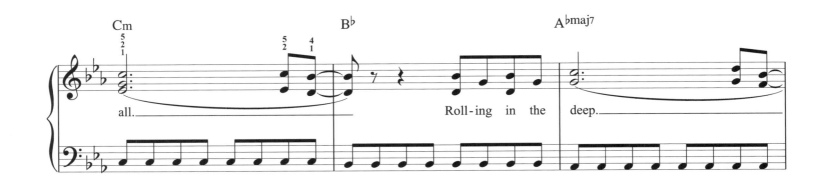

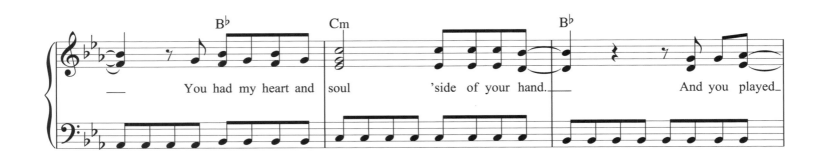

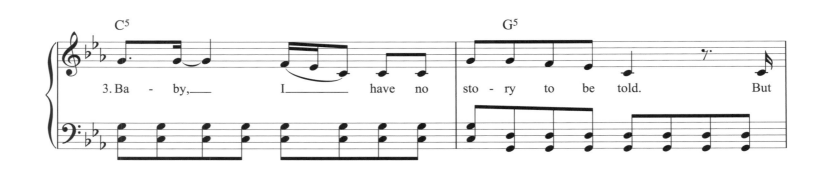

40

Think of — me — in the depths of your des-pair.

Make a — home down there as mine sure won't be shared.

D.S. al Coda

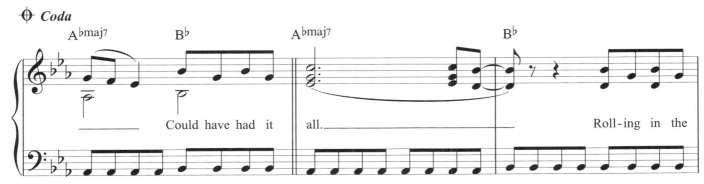

⊕ Coda

— Could have had it all. — Roll-ing in the

deep. — You had my heart and soul — 'side of your hand. —

— But you played — it with a beat - ing.

41

Throw your soul____through ev-'ry o-pen door. Count your_ bless - ings to

find what you look for. Turn my__ sor - rows in - to trea-sured gold. You'll

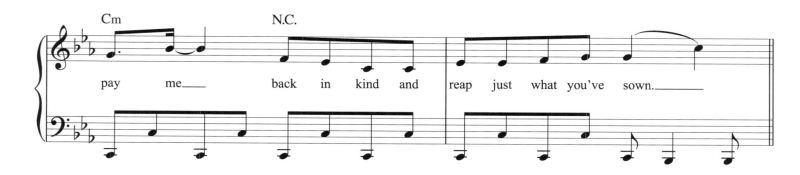

pay me__ back in kind and reap just what you've sown._____

We could have had it all._____

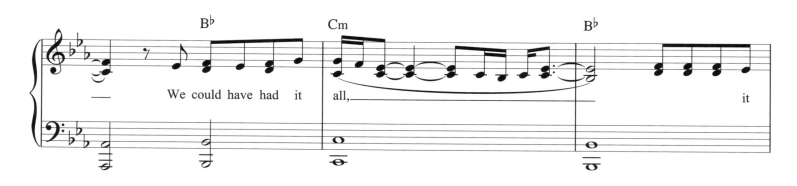

____ We could have had it all,_____ it

Set Fire To The Rain

Words & Music by Fraser Smith & Adele Adkins

48

Someone Like You

Words & Music by Adele Adkins & Daniel Wilson

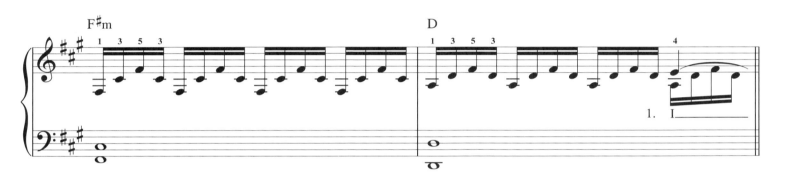

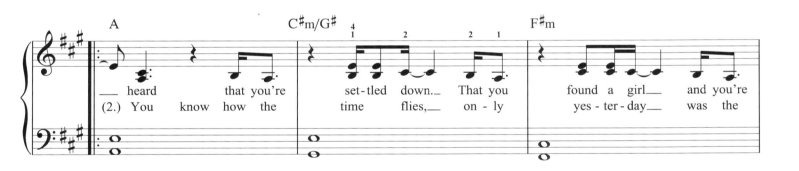

51

1. 3.
F#m D A E
-stead. Some-times it lasts and loves but some-times it hurts in-
8vb
To Coda
F#m D
-stead.
2.
F#m D
-stead.
E/B F#m/C#
Noth-ing com-pares, no wor-ries or cares, re-grets and mis-takes, they are mem-o-ries made.
D5 Bm A/C# D E/D
rit.
Who would have known how bit-ter-sweet this would taste?
a tempo
A E/G# F#m D
Nev-er mind I'll find some-one like you. I wish

noth - ing but the best for you. Don't for -

-get me, I beg. I'll re - mem - ber you said some - times it

lasts and loves but some - times it hurts in - stead.

D.S. al Coda

Coda

53

Turning Tables

Words & Music by Ryan Tedder & Adele Adkins

1. Close e- nough to start a war.
2. Un- der haunt - ed skies I see you.

All that I

Ooh.

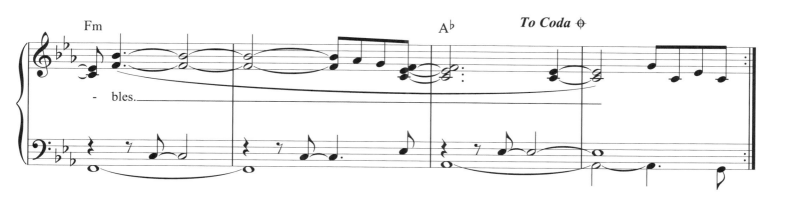

To turn - ing ta -

- bles.

To Coda ⊕

Next time___ I'll___ be brav - er, I'll be___ my___

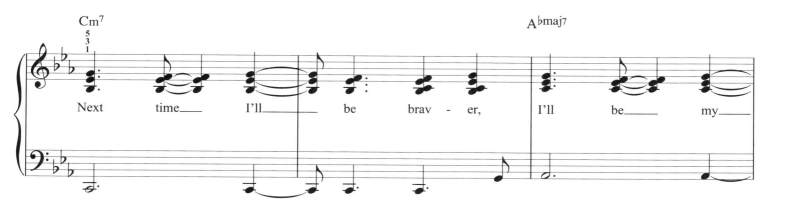

___ own sav - iour, when the thun - der calls___ for me.___

Cm⁷

Next time___ I'll___

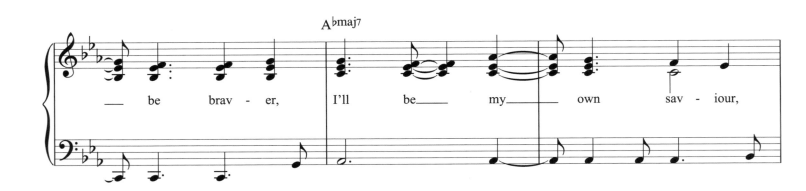

A♭maj7

___ be brav - er, I'll be___ my___ own sav - iour,

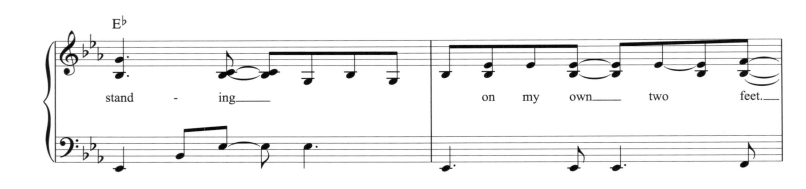

E♭

stand - ing___ on my own___ two feet.___

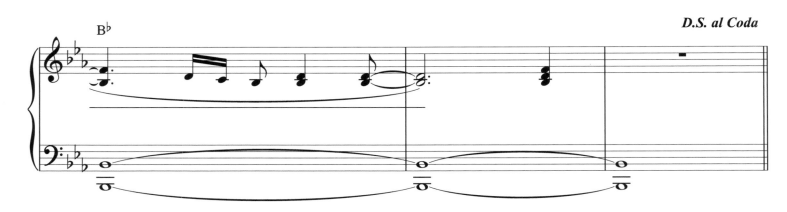

B♭

D.S. al Coda

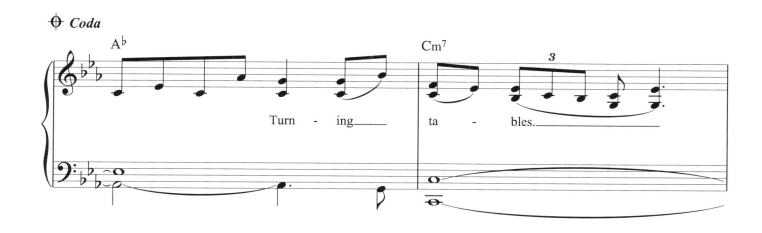

Turn - ing____ ta - bles.____

Take It All

Words & Music by Adele Adkins & Francis Eg White

61

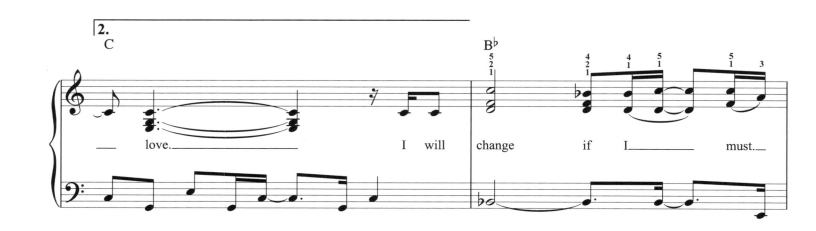

love._____ I will change if I_____ must._

Slow it down___ and bring it home,___ I will ad - just._

Oh, if on - ly,_____ if on - ly you knew___

Free time

that ev - 'ry - thing I do is for_____ you._

62

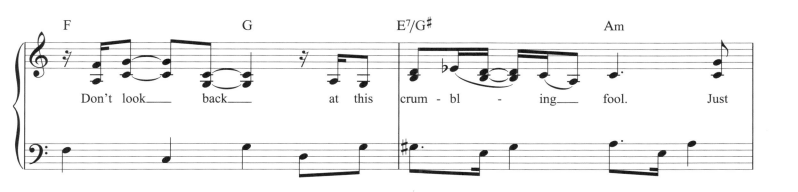

take it,_____ take it all with_ you._____

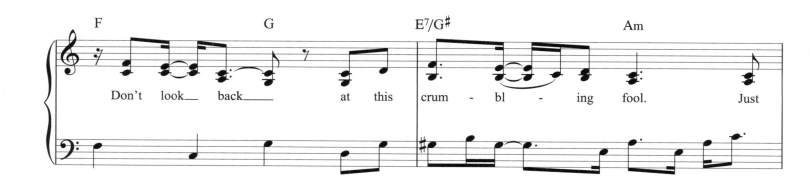

Don't look_ back_____ at this crum - bl - ing fool. Just

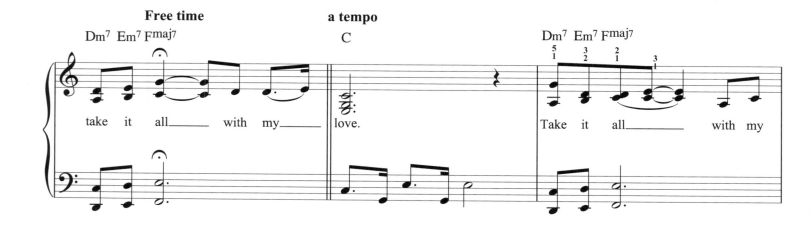

Free time   **a tempo**

take it all___ with my___ love. Take it all_____ with my

love. Take it all_____ with my love.